A Story for a New Journal

Maya sat cross-legged on her bed, the new journal in her lap. Its purple cover glowed softly under the string lights hanging across her room. A little unicorn on the front made her smile. This wasn't just a notebook—it felt like it was waiting for her secrets, dreams, and maybe even the parts of herself she hadn't discovered yet.

At school, Maya always felt like she was caught in the middle. Not the shyest girl, not the most popular, just… Maya. Sometimes she worried that being "in the middle" meant she didn't shine. Her best friend, Lila, had already joined the drama club and was busy rehearsing for the spring play. Her other friend, Zoe, had started a YouTube channel where she posted silly skits. Maya? She wasn't sure what she was supposed to do.

That night, she opened the journal and wrote one sentence: "What if my story matters too?"

The words surprised her. She doodled stars and hearts around them, then wrote about the way her cat always curled on her homework, about how nervous she felt before speaking in class, about the song she secretly wrote but never showed anyone. The more she wrote, the lighter her heart felt—like she'd found a place where she didn't have to pretend.

A week later, during lunch, Zoe asked, "What are you always writing in that book?"
Maya blushed. She wanted to keep it private, but then she remembered her own question: What if my story matters too?

So she shared one of her journal entries about the funny things her cat did. Zoe laughed until she nearly spilled her drink, and soon Lila joined in too. For the first time, Maya felt like maybe her words could bring joy, even if it was just in small ways.

That night, back in her room, Maya wrote in her journal again. "Today I learned that even small stories can be big enough to matter. And maybe, just maybe, I've found my voice."

Copyright 2025 by Library User Group

All rights reserved. No part of this publication may be reproduced,
distributed, or transmitted in any from or by any means, including photocopying, recording or other electronic or mechanical methods,
without the prior written permisiion of the publisher, except in the
noncommercial users permitted by copyright law. For permission requests, please email the publisher with the subject line "Attention:
 Permissions Coordinator" at: Email: contact#libraryusergroup.com

Ordining Information:
Quantity Sales: Special discounts are available for quantity purchases by corporations, assouciations, and others.
For details, contact the publisher at:
:Email: contact#libraryusergroup.com

For orders from U.S. trade bookstores and wholesalers, please contact contact your distribution channel.

CATPUP JOURNAL

ISBN: 978-1-63553-020-9

JUVENILE NONFICTION / GeneralLITERARY COLLECTIONS / Diaries & Journals

FIRST EDITION

Maya sat cross-legged on her bed, the new journal in her lap. Its purple cover glowed softly under the string lights hanging across her room. A little unicorn on the front made her smile. This wasn't just a notebook—it felt like it was waiting for her secrets, dreams, and maybe even the parts of herself she hadn't discovered yet.

At school, Maya always felt like she was caught in the middle. Not the shyest girl, not the most popular, just… Maya. Sometimes she worried that being "in the middle" meant she didn't shine. Her best friend, Lila, had already joined the drama club and was busy rehearsing for the spring play. Her other friend, Zoe, had started a YouTube channel where she posted silly skits. Maya? She wasn't sure what she was supposed to do.

That night, she opened the journal and wrote one sentence: "What if my story matters too?"

www.ingramcontent.com/pod-product-compliance
Lightning Source LLC
Chambersburg PA
CBHW072137070526
44585CB00016B/1719